Also by Martin Leman
MARTIN LEMAN'S COMIC AND CURIOUS CATS
With words by Angela Carter

MARTIN LEMAN'S BOOK OF BEASTS

WORDS BY COLIN PEARSON

LONDON
VICTOR GOLLANCZ LTD
1980

Paintings © Martin Leman 1980/Text © Colin Pearson 1980
Printed in Italy by A. Mondadori Editore, Verona/ISBN 0 575 02875 0

The Polar Bear

First let us meet the Polar Bear.
He lives in Polar places where
It's never truly sunny.
And for this reason, I suppose,
He's often cold between the toes.
And what about his Polar nose?
It must be rather runny.
I shouldn't think it's very nice
To live among the Polar ice.
But Polar Bears do. Funny.

The Camel

The Camel, on the other hand,
Has lots of sun and lots of sand,
But always feels contrary.
Because she has the hump, you see;
And sometimes two (but never three).
Depending on the number, she
Might be a Dromedary.
I can't recall which one is who;
But either way (one hump or two)
Their tempers never vary.

The Koala

Koala Bears are friendlier far.
You'll find them in Australi-ah;
They're cuddly, cute, and quiet.
They live on eucalyptus trees.
(That's *all* they live on, if you please!)
No chips. No cauliflower cheese.
Well, there's a boring diet!
No nuts to crack, no grapes to peel.
Just eucalyptus every meal!
I wouldn't care to try it.

The Bear

The Bear's not fussy what he eats;
Fresh raspberries or sticky sweets,
　　Whatever makes him fatter.
He sometimes has a doleful air –
An out-of-sorts, *sore-headed* bear.
Is someone sleeping in his chair?
　　Or what can be the matter?
Perhaps he lies awake at night.
Or does his waistline feel too tight?
　　More probably the latter.

The Tiger

The Tiger looks *extremely* fit;
Not overweight one tiny bit;
In tip-top shape for fighting.
He's very fierce. I won't pretend
You'd want a Tiger for a friend.
His teeth are sharpened at the end;
His claws are not inviting.
So if you meet one in the street,
Just say you've got a train to meet,
And maybe you'll be writing.

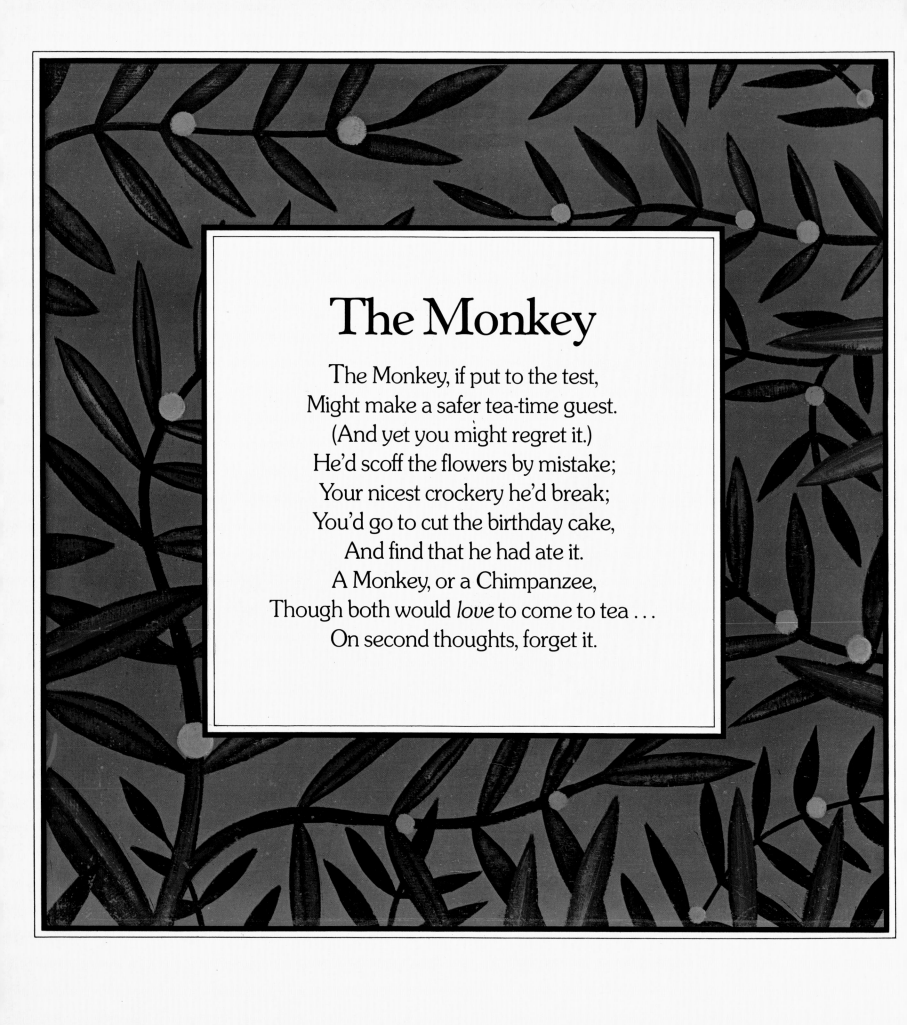

The Monkey

The Monkey, if put to the test,
Might make a safer tea-time guest.
(And yet you might regret it.)
He'd scoff the flowers by mistake;
Your nicest crockery he'd break;
You'd go to cut the birthday cake,
And find that he had ate it.
A Monkey, or a Chimpanzee,
Though both would *love* to come to tea . . .
On second thoughts, forget it.

The Walrus

The Walrus looks, I think you'll find,
More Wal in front, more Rus behind.
(Both ends are pretty fearful.)
He's not a very lovely sight;
His teeth are long and most un-white.
By smiling more perhaps he might
Contrive to seem less tearful.
I think we'd better say Goodbye
Before he really starts to cry.
(I *wish* he were more cheerful.)

The Lioness

The Lioness's sense of smell
(If you're a Zebra or Gazelle)
Should not be taken lightly.
The same goes for the Gnervous Gnu,
The Antelope and Eland, who
Don't stop to say "Well, how d'you do?
O Lioness." (Quite rightly.)
She's resting now, of course – but wait!
That looks distinctly like her mate.
Let's tiptoe off politely.

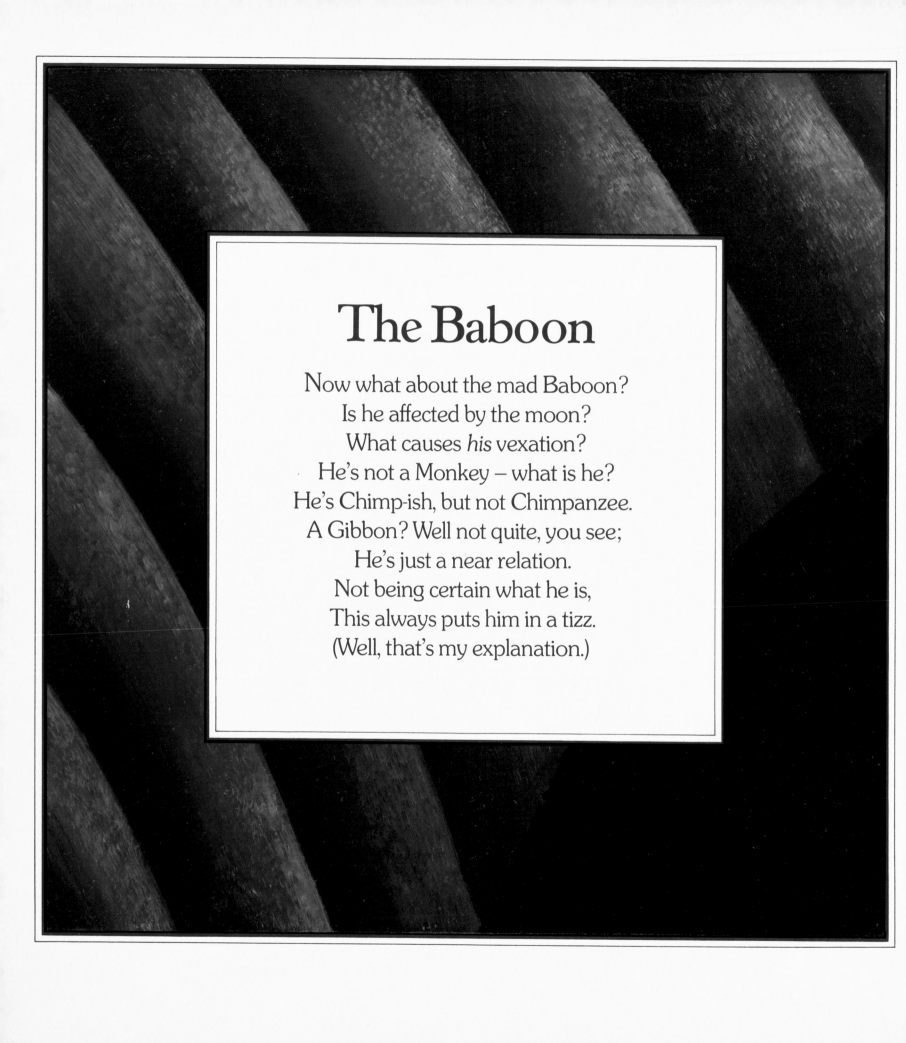

The Baboon

Now what about the mad Baboon?
Is he affected by the moon?
What causes *his* vexation?
He's not a Monkey – what is he?
He's Chimp-ish, but not Chimpanzee.
A Gibbon? Well not quite, you see;
He's just a near relation.
Not being certain what he is,
This always puts him in a tizz.
(Well, that's my explanation.)

The Leopard

The Leopard you would not mistake,
If she popped round to share a cake;
She'd wear a spotted sweater.
A Leopard will not change her spots.
Don't try to hint that polka dots,
Or stripes, or small forget-me-nots,
Might suit her figure better.
In spite of fashion's changing ways,
With spots a Leopard *always* stays.
(If I were you I'd let her.)

The Bison

The Bison is as Bison does.
He's covered in a thick brown fuzz,
And lives upon the Prairie.
All hidden in this thick brown wig,
He's like a sheep, but twice as big;
Well, like a cow (though not a pig)
But very much more scary.
Apart from that, his eyes are small.
You might not see his eyes at all.
(Because he is so hairy.)

The Rhino

The Rhino has no wool at all.
He's covered like a cricket ball,
But very badly fitted.
The seams don't meet upon his flank;
Sometimes he looks more like a tank.
(And if he charges you point-blank,
It pays to be quick-witted.)
But mostly he'll just stand and stare,
And wish he were a Polar Bear
(Who's rather better knitted).